# UNBURDEN YOURSELF

*Ancient Indian Wisdom Simplified*

***Revisiting Bhaja Govindam, a Practical Guide to Vedanta, in the Modern Milieu; Embrace Emptiness to Receive Abundance***

**VOL. 1**

**Dr. K.R.S. NAIR**

***Amazon # 1 bestselling author***

## ALSO BY THE AUTHOR

- **BOUNDLESS POWER OF MINDFUL LIVING**

  *Pamper Your Inner Self, Stay Connected to Spirit and Soar Higher, Grow Inside-Out, and* Reap *the Best of Life.*

- **INCREDIBLE WORD POWER: A UNIQUE HUMAN ENDOWMENT**

  *Know Three Strengths and Four Keys, How to Prudently Script One's Destiny, and Be a Wholesome Winner for Life*

- **THE ART AND SCIENCE OF PRAYER: Why Our Prayers Are Seldom Answered?**

  *Religion, Spirituality, And Science On The Highway To God*

- **What Self-Help Books Won't (& Can't)Tell You**

  *Role of Indomitable Samskara, Vasana, and Karma in Self-Development; Pathfinding to Veritable Happiness & Success*

❖ **GEMS OF MAHABHARATA**

***What's Not in It, You'll Find Nowhere***
***Pearls of Wisdom & Eternal Truths from the Longest Epic, Portrayed in Captivating Style by a Behavioral Scientist***

**VOL. 1** ***VOL. 2*** **VOL.3 VOL.4 VOL.5**

❖ **THE ART OF MAN-MAKING**
***Gita's Timeless Philosophy of Education that Teaches You Manliness is Godliness and the Way to Win the Battle of Life***

**VOL.1 VOL.2 VoL.3**

*Dedicated at the lotus feet of*
*my Guru*
*NavajyothisreeKarunakaraguru*
*of Santhigiri Ashram, Kerala, India*

# TABLE OF CONTENTS

## Dr.K.R.S. Nair

An accredited behavioral science specialist and a corporate trainer with over 25 years of experience, Dr. Nair was the best trainer of SBI.

He had outstanding academic achievements in diverse fields of banking and commerce, business administration, training and development, and animal husbandry.

He received the prestigious Commonwealth Bureau of Animal Health Prize (England) and awards from the Indian Council of Agricultural Research (ICAR), the Indian Society for Training & Development (ISTD), SBI, etc. He was the recipient of the 'Vijay Shree' award (Delhi) and the 'Bharat Mata' award (Kolkata) for a seminal rural development project, which was later rolled out by SBI across the Bank.

***Authored 13 books, of which five have been Amazon's multiple times international # 1 bestsellers***, and the others, # 1 at Amazon India. He also published ten books for SBI's training system, a collection of short stories, about 100 papers, including two internationally acclaimed research papers, more than 140 blog postings, and articles on other popular and management themes, published in reputed magazines like the 'Indian Management'. Contributed articles to the compiled editions published by Kerala Agricultural University, Pentagon Press, Delhi, and Bharatiya Kala Prashasan, Delhi. He is a member of the Bestseller Club of ‘Author Freedom Hub’, a collective of aspiring ‘authorpreneurs’.

Dr. Nair was, for six years, the chief editor of 'Rural Banker', an all-India journal of the State Bank Institute of Rural Development, Hyderabad.

His other cerebral pursuits include papers presented in various international seminars and colloquiums, radio talks, and public speaking on spiritual and management topics.

# PREFACE

*Bhaja Govindam* is an insightful work of Vedanta, presented in a simple and rhythmic style. It comprises 31 verses. The opening stanza is a chorus and chanted at the end of every other verse.

Hailed both as a *stotra* (devotional song) and a *prakarana* (introductory text on spiritual studies), it deals with two-fold motivations of human life – *kanchana* (acquisition of wealth) and *kamini* (enjoyment of lust and wealth); the seer points out the futility of pursuing both. The great saint is urging us to get over our obsession with the trivialities of life and to begin our search for the ultimate Reality, which is the real purpose of life.

At the outset, let's understand that ***the theme of this book is not for the Hindus only. It holds a universal appeal, as it addresses everyone***. The word *'Govindam'* stands for the Atman, which is the Truth behind the ever-changing flux of things that constitutes the universe of our experience. Govinda is the Brahman of the Upanishads and is the highest Reality. So, Bhaja Govindam means seek your identity with the creator, the Brahman, the Supreme.

The text under review is an entry point into Vedanta, which also throws light on many teachings of the scriptures. In a highly simplified form, it distills the teachings of the fundamental texts of Vedanta, Bhagavad Gita, etc. **Attempted here is a thorough study and understanding of the expositions on one of the most popular *stotras* composed by Sankara, which can remove all the delusions of the materialistic world.**

As C. Rajagopalachari said, 'When intelligence matures and lodges securely in the heart, it becomes wisdom. When that wisdom is integrated with life and issues out in action, it becomes devotion. The knowledge that has become mature is devotion. If it does not transform into devotion, such knowledge is useless tinsel.'

# 1

# UNBURDEN YOURSELF

A new training session on spiritual intelligence was in progress.

"In 'Bhaja Govindam', Adi Sankara seems to belittle and ridicule the acquisition of material knowledge. Is it not necessary to gain worldly knowledge as a means of sustenance in life, Sir?"

"Good question, Sandeep. First, let's understand the poem and the context in which the great seer made such a remark," Anandavardhan, the trainer, said.

*"Bhaja/Govindam, bhaja/Govindam,*

*Govindam/bhaja/muda/mate,*

*Samprapte/sannihite/ kale*

*Nahi, nahi/rekshati/dukr'nkarane"*

"Lift the heart to Govinda, lift the heart to Govinda,

Lift the heart to Govinda, O foolish man!

When thou are at death's door,

the rules of grammar that you're trying to master

will not come to your rescue!"

The science you have learned, the books you've studied and mastered, and the skills you have acquired –will any of these stand by you when the death knocks at your door? Could anybody in the world argue with the God of death when He went to them at their appointed time for departure and delay their leaving even by a day or a minute, on the strength of their knowledge? Your erudition, success in life, the wealth you have amassed, the name and fame you have earned, the power you have enjoyed – nothing will come to your rescue when it's time for you to leave this body.

Malathi added: "My Guru used to say: "Your power, education, influence, wealth, etc. will be of no avail in the end. Your friends and relatives can come up to your graveyard only. The only power that can accompany you beyond the graveyard is God, none else".

Anandavardhan continued: "That's why Sankara says, "Worship God". Book learning without devotion to God will be of no avail in the presence of death. The

Acharya warns against wasting all life in mere book learning, neglecting love and devotion to God.

Sandeep raised the doubt of whether Sri Sankara was not belittling worldly knowledge. Certainly not. Chanakya Neethi says: "***To succeed in life, one must learn both worldly knowledge and spiritual knowledge. One cannot just be materially rich and spiritually poor. And, one should not be just spiritually successful while being a worldly failure. Indian wisdom teaches us to be both spiritually and materially developed***".

Isavasya Upanishad also underscores the importance of integrating spiritual knowledge (knowledge gained through experience) and scientific knowledge (amenable to experimentation) for success in life. These two types of knowledge are like the wings of a bird. The bird needs both wings to fly.

## *HOW KNOWLEDGE OBSCURES REALITY?*

Babaji, the guru of Sri M, once told an old holy man, who had great scholarship: "I have great respect for your learning, and more so for the courageous way in which you declined to succeed the head of your Mutt. You have thrown away your *dandi* and crown, and today live like a simple itinerant sanyasin. Great! But you are still far away from the *Brahman* you seek because the burden of knowledge and scholarship that you carry on your head acts as an effective barrier to your understanding of 'Reality.' Shall I continue?"

"Yes, please do. I am beginning to grasp what you are saying."

"***You are so full of knowledge that you have acquired, that there is no space to receive the 'Truth,' which is waiting to enter. Unburden yourself. Throw away all that and embrace emptiness, so that you can receive (the Truth) in abundance.***"

The above episode explains why Sankaracharya chided the old man reciting the lessons of grammar.

Now, over to the context in which this poem was composed. One day, Sri Sankara was walking along a street in Varanasi, followed by his disciples. He heard the sound of grammatical rules being recited by an OLD scholar. Taking pity on the old man, Sankara went up to him and advised him not to waste his time on rules of grammar but to turn his mind to God in worship and adoration. The Hymn to Govinda was composed by the Master on this occasion.

The content has to be discerned in the backdrop of its context. The old man was trying to master the rules of grammar at a time when he should have tuned his mind to revel in the glory of the Lord. ***The pride of learning is a major delusion of the heart***. The Acharya was warning against it.

Malathi: "What is the meaning of the last word 'dukringkarane' in the first stanza of 'Bhaja Govindam', Sir?"

Anandavardhan: "It is a grammatical formula from the *Dhatupatha* in Panini's work on grammar. It stands for all grammatical formulas, or rather for all secular pursuits that do not involve any occupation with God.

In the Chandogya Upanishad, there is a story of Narada seeking instruction from Sanatkumara. In response, Sanatkumara wanted Narada to tell him what he already knew. Narada replied by giving a long list of the sciences and the arts, starting with the Vedas and going down to snake-charming and the fine arts. In his long list, grammar was accorded a prominent place by the sage, as it is considered as the 'Veda of the Vedas'. This is because it is through grammar that one understands the Vedas, by analyzing the words, etc.

However, all the disciplines, of which Narada was a master, were termed by Sanatkumara as names only. The Infinite, Brahman, exceeds all others, and it is in the Infinite that true happiness lies, not in the finite. Thus grammar may be useful as a means for understanding the truth, but it ought not to be reckoned as an end in itself.

If even expertise in grammar or linguistic analysis ('Veda of the Vedas') will not give solace to one at the time of death, what can other disciplines of knowledge do? In the *Ulladu Narpadu* (Forty Verses on Existence) Ramana Maharshi says: "Those people who have an intense fear of death seek as their refuge only the feet of the great Lord, who is without death and birth. **Bondage to what will perish is not the way to get released; the only means for it can be devotion to the imperishable**".

Supriya: "Sir, I have a doubt. Instead of worshipping God always, will it not be okay if one keeps in mind to dwell on the thoughts of God when he is on the deathbed?"

Anandavardhan: "No. Many who have little time for meditating on God in everyday life, often think that they would invoke the Almighty's blessings during the twilight stage of their life. This is not true. The reason: **The thoughts predominant during one's heydays will only occur at the time of death. It will be impossible to turn one's mind towards God when death approaches, notwithstanding the best intention, if he has**

**not prepared himself for it through habitual devotion and worship**. In Bhagavad Gita, Lord Krishna says: "And, at time of death, he who remembers ME alone and departs the body attains My being, there is no doubt in this" *The force of the opening word "And" here implies that* ***unless one has been consistent in remembering God in life, one cannot think of Him at the time of death.***

Sujatha also chipped in with a query. "We know that Sankaracharya's words are indisputably true. Whatever one's level of education, wealth, power, or position, nothing will ever stand in the face of death. We also find that truly blessed people who depart life remembering God have a peaceful death thanks to their unwavering faith and devotion. Although this is a fact of life, people consistently go after material pursuits, often deviate from dharma, and give lesser importance to praying to God. Is it not an irony of human life; why is it so, Sir?"

Anandavardhan: "That's a good question. In the answer to this puzzle lies the secret of human birth. Suppose you plant the seed of a mango in the soil. What plant will grow from that seed? A mango tree only, isn't it? Can you expect to get an apple tree from it? Never. Because, as the seed, so the plant; as the plant, so the fruit. This we know for sure. It is a universal law; universal laws are eternal and are unchangeable.

Now, when it comes to human birth, how does this natural law operate? ***Scriptures say that creation (ulpatthi) will happen as per the karmagati. It means a jiva's birth will occur by the cumulative effect of the karmas accumulated by it over the past.***

Sandeep: "What are the factors governing the karmagati, Sir?"

**Karmagati of any *jiva* comprises three parts. Karmas accrued by a person over the past lifetimes is one. Secondly, similar accumulation of karma by that individual's ancestors over their lifetimes. Thirdly, the influence of the deities worshipped by oneself** and **one's ancestors over generations. Together, these three types of karmagatis go to determine a *jiva*'s birth after death.**

"Would you please explain it, Sir?"

"Okay. First, let's understand the past karma of a person. Any thought arising in one's mind, the words s/he utters, and his/her actions all constitute a person's karma. A karma constitutes a cause and there invariably will be a corresponding effect for it. That's why the law of karma is known as the law of cause and effect. As you sow, so shall you reap. It's again a universal law. What you reap today may be the fruit of a karma you had sown, even in a distant lifetime".

"Is there any time limit for the fruition of one's karma?"

"No. No karma is self-extinguishable. As Newton's third law of motion would tell, for every action, there is an equal and opposite reaction. **Karma will never miss the address of its doer, for which time and space are immaterial.** That's what we find in the story of Bhishma of Mahabharata".

Malathi: "Please tell that story, Sir"

"Bhishmacharya was felled by the arrows of Arjuna on the tenth day of the Kurukshetra war. He didn't die immediately. There was this boon given by his father that he would die only when he wanted to (*iscchamruthyu).* He preferred to leave the body at the commencement of *uttarayana* (the auspicious moment of movement of the sun to the north of the equator). Can you imagine how long did he wait for that moment to arrive? 58 nights!! Remember, Bhishma was lying on a bed of arrows that pierced all over his body.

Because he had a unique spiritual power that enabled him to look at his past lives, Bhishma examined 100 of his earlier births to find the cause of his present suffering. But he remained clueless. When Lord Krishna visited him, the grandsire shared this helplessness with him.

Krishna said: "You reviewed 100 past births. Go further back".

Bhishma replied: "I can't see beyond that"

Krishna said: "I can. As a royal prince in one of the earlier births, you did a mischief during a hunting expedition. In the forest, you saw a moving snake and caught it from behind at its tail. Lifting the reptile and swirling it above your head swiftly, you threw it afar. It landed on a bush of thorny shrubs. With the thorns pierced all over its body, the snake lay there for several days and had a slow and agonizing death. You are reaping the fruit of that mindless karma now.

## *MAJOR LEARNING POINTS*

- ***None of your material accomplishments will come to your rescue when death knocks at your door. Friends and relatives can come up to your graveyard only. Beyond that, your only companion will be God, the Almighty.***

- ***Indian wisdom teaches us to be both spiritually and materially developed.***
- ***Unless one has been consistent in remembering God in his life, one cannot think of him at the time of death.***
- ***Knowledge acts as a barrier in perceiving the 'Reality.'***
- ***Creation will happen only in accordance with the karmagati. And, karmagati has three parts, as detailed in the text.***
- ***No karma is self-extinguishable. It is not limited by time or space.***

2

# KARMAGATI

When the trainer narrated the story of the cause of Bhishma's suffering on the deathbed of arrows, an awestruck Sandeep wondered: “A karma delivering its fruit to its originator after more than a hundred of subsequent births? Unbelievable!"

Anandavardhan: "Yes. As Osho said, science has not come even close to detecting anything like ***the law of karma, which is inescapable and invincible. It never misses its target, i.e., the soul that caused the karma while being in a certain physical body, notwithstanding the number of births and deaths it has had***".

Supriya: "By the way, Sir, how long will a jiva or soul stay in the other world before it re-enters a new body on earth?"

Anandavardhan: "In *Autobiography of a Yogi*, its author's guru Sri Yukteswar, who resurrected before Yogananda tells him: "A person dwells on the astral planet for a certain period, determined by the weight of his material karma that draws him back to the terrestrial realm of a lawfully fixed time. Some souls, after leaving a body, return to earth immediately, usually because of their strong desire to do so. The average length of astral embodiment for fairly advanced persons is from 500 to 1000 years (measured in terms of terrestrial standards of time)... exceptional persons live on an astral sphere for about 2000 years". He also said that **the mere presence of a body signifies that its existence is made possible by unfulfilled desires**.

To revert to our topic, we have discussed the first ingredient of the karmagati that determines the soul's reincarnation, which is a person's accumulated karma in his/her individual capacity. The second part or factor is the yet-to-be-discharged karma of one's ancestors. We all have a long line of forefathers behind us, extending back to many generations".

Thomas: "What is meant by ancestor worship?"

Trainer: "It is the custom of venerating deceased ancestors who still are considered a part of one's family. Their spirits, it is believed, have the power to intervene in the affairs of the living. According to Wikipedia, in European, Asian, African, and some other cultures, the goal of the ancestor veneration is to ensure their continued well-being and positive disposition towards the living, and sometimes to ask for special favors or support. Such veneration remains an integral part of various religious practices in modern times. ***Ancestor worship is considered even more important than the worship of God because a person is indebted to his lineage for his physical birth"***.

Lal: "What is *pitrudosha*, Sir?"

Trainer: "Pitrus are the souls of departed ancestors of one's family. They wait to be reborn and affect their descendants' lives in different ways. This happens because the only source they can look upon for spiritual support for reincarnation is their descendants. *Pitrudosha* is recognized by the signals or messages sent by these deceased ancestors to their living descendants, which may take the form of diseases, sufferings, hardships, and obstacles in everyday life.

***It has to be understood that a person suffers not only from his/her individual past; the suffering also stems from the karma of one's ancestors and will be transmitted to the individual's offspring as well.***

## *You are a crowd-in-one*

In his book titled 'Karma' Sadhguru says that being a product of many influences, each one of us is a crowd-in-one. When there is a pull of accumulated karmic baggage–*sanchita karma* –within an individual, enlightenment and transformation become difficult or impossible. This, according to the author, is because transformation requires a form that is not an amalgam of karmic imprints and influences from a multiple of forefathers. *Crowds can get evolved whereas individuals can get enlightened and transformed.*

*In the context of Bhaja Govindam, we can see that this is another reason why, despite being convinced that daily worship of God is of supreme importance, people, as individuals, fail to get enlightened and transformed. Influenced by the sanchita karma of multiple ancestors, and reveling in the grossly alluring material world, they get transformed themselves from human beings to human 'doings'. The latter connotes craving for sensual pleasures, material possessions, and secular pursuits.*

Suppose someone takes a firm resolve, after studying 'Bhaja Govindam, 'that he would earnestly follow the advice of the great Master and make desirable changes in his way of living. He might be successful in the effort for a couple of days. But soon after, he would slip to the same old rut (human doings) that he was previously in. His old patterns take up the reins of his life.

***As the karmic substance builds up, the discerning mind loses its power of discrimination; it continues to work mainly by habits, patterns, and cycles.*** There lies the overwhelming power of karma. Moreover, people are increasingly inclined to follow their karmic patterns wherein they experience a false sense of safety and better comfort.

Malathi: "Sir, my Guru says that children will be born in a family in accordance with the particular sign of zodiac in which the pitrus remain stationed. Naturally, the manes have to be kept venerated for the well-being of the living".

Anandavardhan: "Right. So, in nutshell, these ancestors who lived according to their individual likes and dislikes, as dictated by their own karmagati, and left behind their share of positive and negative karmas, add to the karmic baggage of their descendants.

Now, let's move to the third aspect of karmagati of a soul, which is the influence of the deities worshipped by a person and the line of ancestors behind him for several generations. Do you know who these deities are?"

Sunita: "The celestial beings: devas and devis".

Trainer: "Not only devas and devis. Our ancestors also used to worship demonic spirits, yakshas, kinnaras, gandharvas, ghosts, etc. These forces will continue to exert their influence on the living descendants of the ancestors. These entities will not allow their worshippers to go above their level and attain enlightenment and transformation. ***Demi gods, evil spirits, etc., once worshipped and prayed to, will exert their control and influence over you even after your death***.

## *Body, an abode of God and demi gods*

Our bodies are the abodes of Supreme Self and also demi gods. They live within us as our organs and are inseparable parts of our existence. Through our actions and offerings, we nourish them and support them. And they reciprocate by fulfilling our desires and protecting us".

Suhra: "But what happens to these gods within us when we die? Do they also perish along with us?"

Trainer: "The deities within us are immortal, and when we die they simply leave our bodies in a subtle form, along with our breath, and return to their astral spheres. But these gods do not want us to be immortal like them. Because, they want us to be always at their disposal – serving, supporting, and nourishing. For that reason, they make sure that we remain subservient to them in our subsequent births as well."

Sandeep: "Why we will remain subordinated to them when we take birth again?"

Trainer: "In Bhagavad Gita, Lord Krishna says:

*"Yanti/devavrata/devan/pitrun/yanti/pitruvrata:*

*Bhutani/yanti/bhutejya:yanti/madyajino'pi mam"*

(9.25)

'It means: The votaries of devas go to devas; to the manes go those devoted to the manes. The worshippers of the elemental gods go to the elementals. And, My worshippers come to Me'.

As you think, so you become. As a result of worship and devotion with single-pointed attention for sufficiently long time, the devotees get their desires fulfilled through the powers they constantly meditate upon. Resultantly, these worshippers ultimately go to the powers so worshipped. To repeat: ***once you are devoted to a god or demi-god,***

***you reach and stay under that power when you die and continue the same worship when you reincarnate.***

Elsewhere in the Gita (7.23), Krishna cautions: 'Men of meager understanding, however, receive limited results. Devotees of lower gods go to those gods. Devotees who worship Me, come to Me (the Infinite One).

Suhra: "Why, despite such unequivocal statements in the Gita and other scriptures, Hindus worship multitudes of gods, Sir?"

Anandavardhan: "Notwithstanding the loud and clear message spelt out in the Vedas, Upanishads, Bhagavad Gita, and by acharyas like Sankara that all the worships and prayers should go to the one and only Infinite-One, people go after demi-gods because, as Sankara says, they lack the knowledge and the power of discrimination due to the specific impressions acquired in previous lives. Wherefrom do they acquire such impressions? Obviously, from their karmagati.

Sadhguru has given an explanation for this phenomenon: "Religion has filled the gap between that blissful state that one can achieve in his nature and his present level of instability. Most people are looking for solace, not liberation. Solace is like a tranquilizer– it puts you to sleep".

Now, let me sum it up. ***The accumulated karma of the self, the ancestors, and the influence of the deities worshipped by the line of ancestors go to constitute the total karmagati of a person, in accordance with which a soul reincarnates on earth***. No two individuals will have the same karmagati. Naturally, their likes and dislikes, mental disposition, and other attributes will differ.

## *Empty your cup to know the 'Truth'*

The foregoing is the major reason why, despite knowing the futility of empirical life and its accomplishments, people go after secular pursuits and pay little attention to worshipping the Almighty. Their power of discrimination gets lost when it comes to knowing the Absolute Truth because of the specific impressions acquired in previous lives. Another reason, as we have seen in the last session, is that accumulation of worldly knowledge, by itself, causes a hindrance to understanding the Absolute Truth. Isavasya Upanishad says: 'he who worships knowledge goes to greater darkness'.

Thomas: "Is it not an irrational statement, Sir? How can the knowledge-worshipper go to greater darkness?"

Anandavardhan: "Remember, in the last session we listened to the conversation between Babaji, the spiritual Master of Sri M, and a learned holy man. The man told Babaji: "I have often wondered what the *sloka* –'he who worships knowledge enters into greater darkness'- from the Isavasya Upanishad, really means," said the monk, "and have never accepted the conventional explanation that 'knowledge' here means the *Apara Vidya* or non-essential knowledge and so on. The *rishis* were very direct and would have used the word *Apara,* if that was what they intended to convey. Now, I am beginning to understand. Pray continue, Sir"

Babaji said, "You are right. The word *Apara* was not used because it was not necessary to qualify *Vidya.* The fact is knowledge, by itself, is an obstacle to understanding the Absolute Truth. I'll explain. You see, when I set out to acquire knowledge of something, what is the process involved? First I observe, then understand it, and then, store it in my memory, right?"

"Yes, Sir."

"When I say that I have knowledge of x or y, what I actually mean is that having understood something, it is now stored in my memory, and I can recall it instantly. This is what constitutes knowledge, any knowledge. So, **all knowledge is memory, and memory, the very word, means, it is a thing of the past**. In the present, there is no memory. Memory is stored information, and is always in the past. Can you, with your keen intelligence, follow what I am saying?"

"Yes."

"Now, 'Truth' cannot be something in the past. It is the 'eternal present,' and therefore, cannot be stored in the memory, which is a thing of the past, the dead past. ***'Truth,' on the other hand is in the present, the now, eternally flowing, pulsating with life, and therefore, cannot be touched by knowledge*.**"

Babaji thus decoded the much misunderstood *Ishvasyasloka.*

Oscar Wilde said: 'Be yourself, everyone else is already taken'.

## ***MAJOR LEARNING POINTS***

- ***The law of karma is inescapable and invincible.***
- ***A person suffers from his individual past, the karmagati of his ancestors, and the deities worshipped by them all.***
- ***Demi-gods, evil spirits, etc. once worshipped, will exert their influence over you even in your later births.***
- ***All the prayers and worships should go to the one and only Infinite Almighty. However, due to the karmic impressions acquired over the past lives, people lose their power of discrimination in the matter and go after demi-gods and deities of all nomenclature.***
- ***Absolute Truth can be comprehended only when all the acquired knowledge and scholarship are removed, providing space for the Truth to enter.***

3

# 'WELL OF WISDOM'

"What comes first, knowledge or wisdom?" And what's the difference between the two?"

Trainer: "What you people are gaining in this classroom is knowledge. It typically comes from books, TED talks, research works, interaction with knowledgeable people, etc. Wisdom is the display of discernment and judgment backed by knowledge and experience. One can say that knowledge is gained from outside the self, whereas wisdom comes from your inside.

Wisdom involves perspective and the ability to make sound judgments about something. "Knowledge is 'knowing' *what* to say; wisdom is knowing *when* and *how to say it."* You would have heard about the 'fruit salad philosophy'. We know that tomato is a fruit. That is knowledge. But we also know that tomatoes will not be put in fruit salad. That is wisdom.

Now, about the question which comes first; knowledge, of course. **Wisdom is developed from knowledge. In other words, knowledge is the raw material for making wisdom**. Without raw materials, the product will not be made. You cannot be wise without being knowledgeable. At the same time, simply because you are knowledgeable does not mean you are also wise."

Supriya: "Sir, is there a relationship between education and wisdom?"

Anandavardhan: "Albert Einstein famously said, "Wisdom is not a product of schooling, but of the life-long attempt to acquire it". It is one of that journey-not-destination sort of things. There is no limit to acquiring wisdom."

Sandeep: "Does time impact wisdom?"

Trainer: "Both knowledge and wisdom are said to increase over time, but time has a more important and direct correlation with knowledge than the other. Generally speaking, ***more time means more knowledge, but more time does not guarantee more wisdom***. Someone may make the same mistake at 60 that he made at 20. It is because knowledge is often a passive acquisition of information, data, or facts, but until the person processes knowledge ('the raw material') he gained with his experience, discretion, judgment, and intuition ('processing'), he doesn't become wise."

Thomas: "Can time negatively affect knowledge and wisdom?"

Anandavardhan: "It's possible. Facts and data can change over time or become outdated; so also, forgotten. However, wisdom tends to be less negatively affected. But as wisdom is subjective and context-based, one may become out of touch with the changing times and become less wise. Compared with the yesteryears, the practical wisdom of people seems to be better in modern times. For instance, in the olden days, the wise solution for an unwanted pregnancy was mostly a quick marriage; in modern times, a wise choice could mean abortion or embracing single parenthood."

Lal: "Tell us more about the practical application of wisdom, Sir."

Trainer: "As we discussed, knowledge is 'externally sourced' from books, videos, training, etc.; ***wisdom arises primarily from 'internal sources' like introspection, intuition, analysis, judgment, etc***.

**Whereas knowledge is not necessarily guided or enhanced by wisdom, wisdom cannot**

**be acquired and applied without knowledge**. At the same time, its application often requires much more than mere facts to perceive and choose the right action or to avoid the wrong action or decision. The internal sources that build up wisdom include intuition, feelings, moral or ethical values, and the like.

*Knowledge* has a 'theoretical approach' whereas wisdom entails a 'spiritual approach'. The former is associated with the mind, and the latter, with the soul. In the Bhagavad Gita, Lord Krishna tells Arjuna:

"*Iti/te/jnanamakhyatam, guhyat/guhyataram /maya*

*vimrusyaitadaseshena, yetechasi/tata/kuru*"

(18.63)

At the end of his lengthy discourse on 'karma yoga', 'jnana yoga', and 'bhakti yoga', Krishna says that He has thus imparted the knowledge about what is right and what is wrong, and advises Arjuna to reflect on what the Lord said. It sends out the message that any extent of *listening* (read, acquiring knowledge) will not make one wise. As Swami Chinmayananda says, the knowledge gained through reading or listening has to be assimilated and brought within the warp and the woof of one's understanding for it to get converted into wisdom. Therefore, Arjuna is asked not to straightaway accept whatever Krishna told him as Truth, but to independently and critically think over all that the Lord has declared. Reflection, observes Chinmayananda, is 'putting the ideas between the mind and the intellect and chewing them properly' to churn out wisdom. The recipient of the knowledge will have to get his confirmation from his bosom.

In *Vivekananda A Born Leader,* author Asim Chaudhuri writes: "**Just as data is not useful until it is transformed into information, knowledge is not complete until it is developed into wisdom.** To get a little further, if you package knowledge, experience, discretion, and intuitive understanding, and include the ability to apply these qualities effectively toward finding solutions to problems, you can write "wisdom" in bold letters outside the package."

Supriya: "Sir, what is the difference between wisdom and insight?"

Trainer: "Insight refers to the ability to see and understand clearly the inner nature of things, especially by intuition. While insight and wisdom are very close concepts, insight involves a bigger picture than wisdom."

Suhra: "Can knowledge ever be an obstacle to wisdom?"

Anandavardhan: "Yes, it's possible too. In some instances, too much knowledge may act as a hindrance to wisdom, as we have seen in the verse from Isavasya Upanishad in the last session. For example, some people may be overconfident about their learning and experience and refuse to consider other perspectives or ideas because they think, "I'm OK, you're not OK". As a result, they become unable to make appropriate decisions. Similarly, if you rely too much on experience and are unwilling to adapt to new situations, your knowledge may stand in the way of seeking the best possible solutions. In all such situations, a wise person will understand the limits of his knowledge and will be open to learning from others.

Sandeep: "Sir, does one acquire wisdom proportionate to his learning? Like, the more educated you are, the more wise you are?

Anandavardhan: "No. It is possible to have wisdom without having much learning or education. For, ***wisdom comes from life experience, observations, reflections, and a deep understanding of oneself and the world at large***. Let's move to a story:

There was an educated, miserly man. His wife was very generous, but she didn't have access to her husband's money. They were very rich and could easily have helped their villagers, who were generally of poor means. For months together, the villagers suffered from drought and famine. They could not cultivate on the dry land for want of irrigation facilities. Shortage of food and malnutrition resulted in many deaths.

The wife begged the husband to dig one or two wells in the village so that people could have drinking water and irrigation facilities. But the miserly husband didn't budge. The wife thought: 'Who knows, I can perhaps try to dig a well and get water for the needy'. She asked one of their servants to help her dig a well at a suitable place. She also joined him in the task. Every day, they went on digging, but there was no sign of water. The husband laughed at the lady and said: "You continue digging for a year, but won't get water in this ground. Only the well of your stupidity will get deeper by day, I tell you".

The lady and the servant were not disappointed and continued the digging. The husband went to the spot every day and continued mocking their 'futile' effort. One day, the servant told the lady: "Mother, we're working hard, but the master is being unsympathetic and continues ridiculing us. If you'll permit, we'll play a trick."

"Like what?"

The servant said: "Every morning, your husband comes here and laughs at our effort in this noble task. Tomorrow, before he comes, let us pour some oil on the ground inside the pit. When he sees the oil in the area dug, your husband will be very excited, I'm sure. Who knows, perhaps he will draft more workers to dig deep on the spot with the hope of harvesting oil from underneath. With more people to complete the task of digging the well, our purpose will get served, I hope".

The woman agreed.

The following day, the husband, as usual, went to see the progress of the 'well of stupidity' and was astonished at what he saw in the wet sand brought out from the pit – a thick consistency of oil! He could not believe his eyes. Excited, he thought: 'Here's a golden treasure in my ground. I want to take credit for discovering oil here'. After a moment of thought, he asked his wife: "Will you go to the market and get something for me urgently? You may take the servant along with you to carry the things bought. Don't worry about this work here. I will immediately arrange for more workers to complete this digging work for you."

Accordingly, the lady and the servant went to the market to buy the things that the husband wanted them to get. As soon as they disappeared from the scene, the man summoned 20 workers and asked them to dig at the work site for the treasure he had in mind. While they were on the job, the greedy man waited by the side with great expectations and plans. After a few hours of digging, the workers hit the water. They were thrilled, and their master was devastated, seeing a spring of water coming up in spurts all around the new well!

Distraught, the man thought: "Who wants water? I wanted oil so that I could sell it and become richer and richer. For me, what use is there for more water other than giving it free to the villagers?"

In the meanwhile, his wife and the servant returned from the market. They were delighted at what they saw at their work site. It was a dream-come-true for the lady and her servant. The husband, who could not hide his emotions, said, "I don't understand this! This morning only, we saw clear signs of oil underneath the ground. I hired the workers to get to the oil well, but they struck water only!"

Tongue in her cheek, the beaming lady said, "Money and the might of learning gave way to the well of wisdom".

"What do you mean?" the man asked.

His wife said, "Where there is a will, there will be a way to a well. Our servant's well of wisdom brought us a well of water today. God wanted you to help the needy; not to remain greedy".

(Adapted from 'Tales of Wisdom' by Sri Chinmoy)

## *MAJOR LEARNING POINTS*

- ***Knowledge comes from outside, wisdom comes from inside.***
- ***More time means more knowledge, but not more wisdom.***
- ***Wisdom cannot be acquired and applied without knowledge.***
- ***Knowledge is not complete until it is developed into wisdom.***
- ***Wisdom arises from life experiences, observations, reflections, and a deep understanding of the self and others.***

## 4

# DISCRIMINATION IS THE KEY

Trainer: "Our great Acharyas of yore have stressed the importance of developing discrimination between the Real and the unreal in life. It is because, among living beings, only humans have the endowments of conscience and self-awareness, besides independent will and imagination, to understand the futility and dangers of pursuing the unreal.

The verse 2 of 'Bhaja Govindam' says:

*"Mudha/jaheehi/dhanagamatrishnam,*

*Kuru/sadbuddhim/manasi/vitrishnam*

*Yallabhase/nijakarmopaattam*

*Vittam/tena/vinodaya/chittam"*

"Fool! Give up this insatiable craving for wealth

Be wise and develop serene content;

Be satisfied and happy with the fruits of your own work"

Is Sankara saying to give up wealth? Nobody can misconstrue it that way, for the advice is "*jaheehi dhanagama trishna*"- give up the insatiable longing to amass wealth. What is to be detested is only the *greediness* for acquiring more and more wealth – money and material assets of all kinds"

Thomas: "Why one should not long for more and more wealth? How can it be a bad thing, especially in an uncertain world?"

Anandavardhan: "In Kattopanishad (1,27) Nachiketas tells Yamadharma: "*na vittena tarpaneeyo manushyo....*". It means men will never be satisfied with wealth. Craving for more money and wealth is like adding firewood to a burning fire. The fire will never be satiated and will want you to feed it again."

Sandeep: "But Sir, if one should not acquire more wealth, how can one have a comfortable and secure life, free of tensions?"

Trainer: "The latter part of the same stanza of 'Bhaja Govindam' answers that question, Sandeep. "*Yellabhase nijakarmopaattam vittam*"- 'what you earn by your own labor' *"tena vinodaya chittam"*- 'enjoy that and be content with it'. So goes the wise counsel of the Acharya.

The simple and profound truth that the said stanza expounds is that the insatiable longing to acquire wealth has to be eschewed at all costs. Then only lasting peace and happiness will be achieved".

The Acharya then talks about another equally or more ruinous or intractable natural inclination of people, especially the youth, i.e., 'lust'. The third stanza says:

*"Naaristanabharanabhidesam*
*Drstva/ma /ga/mohavesam*
*Etanmamsavasadivikaram*
*Manasi/vichintaya/varam/varam."*

"Excited by women's beauty, her bosom, and the region of navel do not allow yourself to be lost;

They are only forms of mere flesh.

Think of them as such every time you look at them."

Sankara is warning against getting caught in the vortex of lust. It is normal for men and women to get attracted to each other; it is a natural law. But if the attraction towards the opposite sex becomes uncontrollable and you covet a girl or woman who does not belong to you, it will lead to unpleasant results and misery. The way out is to control your senses and urges by exercising wisdom.

Craving for wealth, we found earlier, is a sure recipe for misery; so also, going for bodily pleasures. Sankara cautions not to fall prey to frenzied delusion by seeing the seductive female form. Discrimination is the only way to exorcise this 'evil spirit'.

*"Nareestanabharanabheedesam,*
*drushtua maa gaa mohaavesam...."*

Before casting your covetous glances on women, pause and reflect on what is at the core of the beauty that lures and deludes you. The woman's breast, navel, and other parts that seduce you –are they not mere flesh, blood, and skin? Just as the bones, flesh, blood, and veins are beautifully 'packed' by the outer skin, craving and lust deceptively conceal a core of inevitable pain. Be wise and control your senses. Just look around and see the unenviable plight of the people who easily give in to uncontrolled lust and greed.

Swami Vivekananda said: "We are like moths plunging into the flaming fire, knowing that it will burn us......"***Desire is never satiated by enjoyment***; enjoyment only increases desire as butter fed into fire increases the fire". ***Desire is increased by desire.*** Knowing all this, people still plunge into it all the time........"

Swami continues: "Oh, the terrible degradation, the terrible misery of it! What little flesh, the five senses, the stomach! ***What is the world but a combination of stomach and sex?*** Look at millions of men and women – that is what they are living for. Take these away from them, and they will find their life empty, meaningless, and intolerable. Such are we. And such is our mind; it is continually hankering for ways and means to satisfy the hunger of the stomach and sex.......***these desires of the body bring only momentary satisfaction and endless suffering.*** It is like drinking a cup of which the surface layer is nectar, while underneath all is poison. But we still hanker for all these things" (The Complete Works, 8:117-118).

## The essence of spiritual discipline

A man of wisdom will apply his discrimination, think intelligently, and make judicious decisions. In other words, he exercises his head first – 'heady' he is. Secondly, he will be empathetic and engage his emotional intelligence, which is much more important than cognitive (mental) intelligence, and that makes him 'hearty'. Being 'heady' and 'hearty', man becomes humane.

His third vital part is the bosom and the stomach. Although they come after the head and the heart, when the tummy and the sexual needs take precedence over cognitive and emotional intelligence, the man, the only living being walking vertically upright on his two limbs, virtually assumes an inverted posture – the head and heart pushed down to the bottom, and the gut and sex jacked up to the top.

Ramana Maharshi once said: "Mind binds man, and the same mind liberates him. Mind is constituted of *sankalpa* and *vikalpa*- desire and disposition. ***Desire shapes and governs disposition.*** Desire is of two kinds – the noble and the base. The base desires are lust and greed. Noble desires direct us toward enlightenment and emancipation. Base desires contaminate and cloud the understanding. *Sadhana* is easy for the aspirant who is endowed with noble desires. Calmness is the basis for spiritual progress. Plunge the purified mind into the Heart. Then the work is over. This is the essence of all spiritual discipline" {*Face to Face with Sri Ramana Maharshi*, pp.341}.

## ***MAJOR LEARNING POINTS***

- ***Greediness to acquire more and more wealth should be detested. It is like adding more firewood to the burning fire.***

- ***Enjoy what you earn by your own labor and be content with that.***

- ***Be warned against getting into the vortex of lust, which is ruinous.***

- ***Desire is never satiated by enjoyment. It breeds more and endless desire.***

- ***Desire is of two kinds- the noble and the base.***

- ***Base desires are lust and greed; noble desires lead us to enlightenment and emancipation.***

5

# TAKE A CUE FROM THE IMMACULATE LOTUS

Anandavardhan: "The first three stanzas of the 'Bhaja Govindam' talk about the futility of the insatiable quest for acquiring material knowledge, amassing wealth, and the pitfalls of going after sensual pleasures. Indulgent people are blissfully unaware of the ephemeral nature of life and forget that, being endowed with self-awareness and conscience, one's endeavor should always be to realize what is of true value in life."

Sandeep: "But the way many people conduct their lives appears to suggest they hold a view that they are going to live forever."

Trainer: "In Mahabharata, during the Pandavas' exile, Dharmadeva appeared to them in the guise of a crane and asked Yudhishtira a series of 125 questions. Of them, one was: "What is most wonderful?"

The Pandava replied: "Every day, numerous living entities are dying and going to the abode of Yama. Yet one thinks and believes one will live, and remain forever (immortal). What can be more wonderful than this?"

Malathi: "Generations have heard this famous statement of truth by Yudhishtira. But who cares to ponder over it and change their outlook on life and living? As Sir said earlier, it seems to be the impact of the overbearing karmagati in the jiva. ***People just hear, don't listen***. And we continue the craze for acquiring material possessions like wealth, knowledge, sensual indulgence, etc. Yudhishtira's observation about the nature of human beings is quite valid in the modern times as well".

Anandavardhan: "Another plausible reason for the lackadaisical attitude of people in heeding to the sage counsels of the Acharyas is interesting to note. Religious people like the Hindus who believe in rebirth hold on to the notion of '*punarapi/jananam, punarapi/ maranam, punarapi/jananee/jattare/sayanam*'. It means, we live and die again and again, and leave and return to the mother's womb again and again. People holding this view are complacent and think that pursuing lofty goals like deliverance can wait. It can be in the next birth. In this life, they want to indulge in a craving for material possessions and comforts. Like procrastinating things in daily life, they postpone the dividends that could be earned through virtuous living to the next life."

Thomas: (With a smile) "You have a valid point there, Sir. In religions that don't believe in reincarnation, people may have a sense of urgency for spiritual accomplishments and noble goals as they think that the one they have is their only life. No return to the mother's womb."

Lal: "When you adhere to the philosophy of '*punarapi/jananam, punarapi/maranam.......*' you don't find the need to bother whether anybody would cry or not when you die. After all, once you're dead, what difference does it make whether someone would mourn your death or not? That too, when there is the belief that you would reincarnate".

Trainer: "Now, let's move on to the 4th stanza of 'Bhaja Govindam' which is a beautiful poetic expression about the transitory nature of life. The Acharya draws our attention to the regular sight of the petals of a lotus holding drops of water and exclaims:

*"Nalineedhalagatajalamatitaralam,*
*tatvajeevithamathisayachapalam*
*Viddhi/vyadhyabhimangrastam,*
*Lokam/sokahatam/cha /samastam".*

'The water drop resting on a lotus petal has a very precarious existence; so too is life, with its uncertain and unsteady nature. Know that the world is in the grip of disease and anxiety, and is smitten with sorrow.'

The drop of water that has jumped onto the lotus petal from the surrounding waters majestically boasts of an independent existence and gleefully swings hither and thither on the smooth petal. But a strong turbulence in its substratum, which may occur at any time, will throw the water drop back to the surrounding water body, extinguishing its independent existence. Human life is like a dew drop on a lotus leaf that looks elegant and beautiful. One's pride, power, majesty, and the very existence itself could be wiped out within no time and at any time.

After all, what is this life like? In the Yaksha Prasna mentioned earlier, one question that the Yaksha asked Yudhishtira was: "What is the news?" (What is the real situation in the material world?).

The Pandava replied: "The world full of ignorance is like a pan. The Sun is fire, and days and nights are fuel. The months and the seasons constitute the wooden ladle. Time is the cook that cooks all creatures in that pan (with such aids). This is the real news of what is happening in the material world, which is a miserable place full of ignorance".

In his reply, Yudhishtira talks repeatedly about man's ignorance about the reality of the world, which finds elaboration by Sankara in the second half of the stanza under discussion.

## The significance of the lotus in spirituality

Supriya: "Sir, please explain how and why the lotus gained a lot of importance in the world of spirituality?"

Anandavardhan: "Lotus is nature's one of the most mysterious flowers and carries a lot of significance in many cultures. According to many Eastern cultures, it is the most sacred plant in the world. Lotus has a life cycle that is dissimilar to any other plant. Its mysterious nature is such that with its roots latched in the mud, it submerges every night into the water and emerges the following morning in full glory, without even a speck of mud or dirt, sparkling clean. This phenomenon has earned the lotus the name of the flower with a 'rebirth' and a symbol of spiritual enlightenment.

Thanks to its unique features, the lotus is often associated with godly figures in some cultures. For the Egyptians, it represents the universe. The ancient Egyptians believed that lotus could resurrect the dead, as seen in *the Book of the Dead transformation spells*. In the Hindu culture, the lotus is beheld as the seat of gods and goddesses. A longstanding Buddhist story states that the Buddha appeared atop a floating lotus, and his first footsteps on Earth left lotus blossoms.

Once, it is said, Sankaracharya and his disciples were walking on two sides of a river that was in full swell. The Acharya hailed his dearest disciple on the other side of the river: "Sanandana". When he heard his guru calling him from the other side, Sanandanan, out of his deep devotion to the guru, didn't bother about the overflowing river, and started walking across it. Miraculously, his every footstep on the water was supported by a lotus from below till he reached the other shore! Happy at the unusual faith and determination displayed by his disciple, Sankara embraced Sanandanan and called him 'Padmapada' (Padma= lotus; pada=foot), and that was his new name thenceforth.

The lotuses with different colors also have significance. For Buddhist practitioners, a white lotus symbolizes purity, whereas a yellow lotus is associated with spiritual ascension.

## *Unparalleled survival instinct of lotus*

Lotus also has an unbelievable instinct to survive. Its seeds can survive years together without water and can germinate even two centuries later! The flower also blooms in the most unlikely places like the mud of murky river water in Australia and Southern Asia. Aside from finding sanctuary in the muck, the waxy protein layer on its petals helps it re-bloom each morning from underneath the water body, untainted, intact, and in full splendor. Its resurrection every day, as beautiful as in the previous evening, suggests its refusal to accept defeat and its unwavering faith in itself!

## *The lessons for humans*

- Swami Vivekananda said, "Just as water cannot wet the lotus leaf, so work cannot bind the unselfish man by giving rise to attachment to results". The life of a lotus dictates how humans ought to live in this world – ***work persistently, but be not attached to the results and the surroundings***.
- "Just like the lotus, we too can rise from the mud, bloom out of the darkness, and radiate into the world" (Unknown).

- The delicate-looking flower emerges from unlikely conditions of shallow murky waters without a speck of mud on its pure white or pink petals. Despite spending its night immersed in muddy pond water, it bursts forth each morning triumphantly. Likewise, instead of getting disheartened by the heavy 'mud' in your life, focus on the sunshine, look for the blessings tucked into every day, and use them to nourish your soul.
- ***If you are resilient and persevering, notwithstanding the adverse circumstances, you can, and will prosper***.
- Many a time, life will throw mud on your path. Health and work-related issues, financial problems, strained relationships, and social, economic, and family challenges are the muddy life situations we encounter. A strong willpower and firm resolve to overcome difficulties will bring rich dividends.

**"WHEN YOU CHANGE HOW YOU LOOK AT THINGS, THE THINGS YOU LOOK AT WILL CHANGE"**

(Wayne Dyer)

## ***MAJOR LEARNING POINTS***

- ***Like water drop on a lotus petal, human beings have a precarious existence.***

- ***Our material accomplishments, name, fame, pride, power, and the very existence itself could be wiped out at any time.***

- ***Lotus has an unparalleled survival instinct and its life throws out many valuable lessons to us.***

- ***If you are persevering and resilient, notwithstanding the adverse circumstances, you can not only survive, but also prosper and be a victor.***

6

# THE WORLD OF HYPOCRITES

*Yavadvittoparjanasakta*
*Stavannijaparivaro/raktah*
*Pascajjivati/jarjaradehe*
*Vartam/kopi /na/prachhati/gehe (5)*

A rich person will always be surrounded by sycophants who are ever willing to do his bidding. Wherever he goes, he gets showered with love, respect, and readiness to take his orders. But once he loses his wealth and power, nobody bothers to even look at him, let alone respect and love - his family members included. When he becomes older and older, then also people avoid him. They would easily forget all the favors and support he extended to them during his heydays. This is how the world is. During the times of Adi Sankara it was so; in modern times too it is so.

Supriya: "Sir, if the parameter for attracting love and respect is wealth, can people be faulted for their craving for wealth? That being the reality, is not this verse antagonizing the suggestion in the second *sloka* that says, "Fool, give up this insatiable desire for wealth?"

Anandavardhan: "Please understand the meaning of the stanza in full. It says: "As long as you can earn, your kith and kin will remain attached to you. Later on, when your body becomes infirm, no one even at your home will speak to you." This *sloka* is actually buttressing the point the Acharya made earlier regarding the craving for wealth. Will wealth provide security for life? Or, give immortality? Brihadaranyaka Upanishad gives the answer thus:

Sage Yajnavalkya, when he decided to become an ascetic, resolved to divide his property into two halves and give it to his two wives. When she heard about the husband's decision, Maitreyi, his second wife, asked him: "You want to offer me all your wealth? I have a question: 'Can I become immortal through wealth?' Yajnavalkya said: "Far from it. You will be a well-to-do person like any other rich guy, but there is no hope of immortality through wealth". And Maitreyi promptly declined the offer.

Nobody can dispute the Acharya's observations in the said verse. So long as you are wealthy and powerful, your family will love and hover around you. But, once your wealth is lost and you start getting old, your friends and relatives not only don't care for you, they don't even bother to ask you how you are! So, what did they love earlier - you the person, or your money and power? The answer is obvious. The message the *sloka* conveys is that ***the world revolves around quid pro quo***. "Give me something. I'll give you something in return".

Swami Sukhabodhananda has narrated this story:

A king invited a Sufi mystic one day for dinner. At the appointed time, the king and the other invitees, who were great scholars, waited at the dining table for the Sufi mystic to arrive. In the meantime, the Sufi mystic came to the palace gate in ordinary casual wear. Seeing his dress that was simple and unimpressive, the guards at the gate refused him entry inside. The Sufi mystic sensed the reason for their objection and went back. After a while, he returned wearing attire acceptable to the security guards and got entry inside the palace.

The king welcomed him. As soon as he occupied the seat marked for him, the Sufi mystic removed his coat and kept it next to him on the chair. When the food was served, he stood up and reverentially offered it to his coat. Seeing this ridiculous act, the king and the guests were flabbergasted; they all looked at one another. The king asked the Sufi mystic: "Why are you behaving in this silly manner? You're offering the food to your coat?"

The Sufi mystic answered: "What else? I got entry inside this palace only after I wore this coat. It made me understand that the food is served in deference to the coat, not my being".

## *TWO ASPECTS OF HUMAN LIFE*

In the words of Swami Ranganathananda, the 13th President of Ramakrishna Mission, **we have two aspects to ourselves – one, the deeper aspect of 'being' and the other, a superficial aspect of 'function'**. In the aspect of being, we ask ourselves: 'Who am I?" In the aspect of function, the question asked is: "What do I do?"

A wealthy man is seen by others from his functional aspect only. "What can he do for me?" "What will I get from him?" The others are in expectation mode so long as the person is wealthy and powerful. Their love and regard for him emanate from this perceived functional aspect. Once he loses his wealth, the expectation the others have of him also wanes.

According to Ranganathananda, the functional state is a static mode of the mind. A static mode means one which is focused on *process* –"as head of the family, he should protect us because he is rich and capable". In this mode, people are in a *reactive* and *receptive* mode. They nurture anticipations like: "Will he support us?"

***Most of us are so locked up at the function level of our lives that we have lost touch with the being level of ourselves***. That's why we consider the position of a person and his wealth as the yardstick to love him. That's why the Sufi mystic in the story was rejected by the palace guards in the first instance. Sri Sankara laments about this ubiquitous human nature.

Now, look at what happens when a person believes that someone else is higher than himself in wealth, position, or power. His self-esteem starts to erode and he considers himself a victim because he is out of control. A person holding such a belief sooner or later will take away control from the other party as well and will hold the latter in poor esteem. That's what happens when a wealthy person turns poor. It shows that the love and respect the person in victim mode showed to the wealthy guy was directed at his functional state only, and not towards his being level.

What happens when you enter your being stage? There you are in a *dynamic* state and are free of any binding structures like victimization and lack of self-esteem. Mutual respect and esteem originate when there is faith in oneself and faith in others. As Ranganathananda says, those who live only at the level of function, which unfortunately is the case with most of us, become defunct when they cease to be functional. Those who live at the plane of being, and function from that awareness level, never experience being defunct, even when they are out of function, or when they become old and totter on a stick. Reveling in such an awareness, one can pre-empt the world rejecting him; instead, he can reject the world.

What Sankaracharya says is that we're living in a world of hypocrites. He cautions: Don't get attached to your near and dear. You may love them, and take care of them when you are capable of it. Thus far, and no more. Given the nature of the world, attachment will lead to disappointment and misery. For, the family and friends will be around you until you are in command and control.

*That's what the story of Vijay Pat Sanghania tells us. In 1940, he started the Sanghania Company on a very modest scale by manufacturing blankets. A visionary as he was, he expanded to cement, steel, etc. and the Company grew. He became the*

*Chairman and Managing Director of the industrial giant J.K. Group, whose market value rose to Rs. 11,000 crores. Vijay had two sons, Gautam Singhania and Madhupati Singhania. Madhupati picked up quarrels with their father on property issues and left for Singapore for good. Vijay transferred all the shares in the name of Gautam. The son became the Chairman and M.D. of the Group of Companies. From their 37-storied J.K.House, one day Gautam expelled his parents to the streets. The man who was bestowed with Padma Bhushan by the nation, and was honored with the coveted title the Sheriff of Mumbai, at the age of 82, lives destitute in a rented flat in Mumbai, knowing not how to make ends meet!* His autobiography *'An Incomplete Life'* is a telling example of what Sri Sankara describes in the 5th verse of 'Bhaja Govindam'.

The Acharya says: Do not cling to what is ephemeral. Seek the feet of 'Govinda'. "*Govindam bhaja muda mate*".

***The way you direct your thoughts is the way you direct your life.***

## ***MAJOR LEARNING POINTS***

- ***As long as you're earning and wealthy, people will be around you and be ready to do your bidding. Once your wealth drains away, the retinue also will disappear forever.***

- ***The world revolves around quid pro quo. "Give me something; I'll give you something in return."***

- ***We have two aspects to ourselves – one, the deeper aspect of 'being' and the other, a superficial aspect of 'function'. In the former aspect we ask the vital question: "Who am I?" and in the latter aspect, "What do I do?"***

- ***The way you direct your thoughts is the way you direct your life.***

7

# IN THE GUEST HOUSE CALLED BODY

Trainer: "*Bhaja Govindam* started with the futility of book learning without devotion to God, as the pride of learning would alienate one from the path to the Almighty. In the second stanza, the Acharya talked about the craving for money, pointing out that it will only breed pain and sorrow. And he spoke about lust, which is the most intractable of all vices. The ephemeral nature of life was also likened to the unstable water drop dancing on a lotus petal.

Proceeding further, Sri Sankara exposed the hypocritical nature of human beings, who will cling to and hover around wealthy people so long as they remain rich and resourceful, and dump them mercilessly when they are old and infirm.

Sandeep: "Sir, on the whole, is this not portraying a pessimistic view of life that discourages and demotivates people on all fronts?"

Anandavardhan: "Some Western critics also hold on to such a viewpoint. But it has to be understood that ***Indian spirituality is unique in the sense that it evolved from the first-hand experience of our rishis of yore, who deduced the truth of Existence through spiritual visions (darshan) from their relentless pursuit of realizing the Ultimate. Their revelations were experiential, not experimental.*** They understood and declared that all material accomplishments, including garnering knowledge, amassing wealth, seeking sensual pleasures, etc., besides being transitory, will be of little use in realizing the ultimate purpose of life. Clinging to them will not provide lasting peace and happiness.

Look at the next verse, which goes a step further in elucidating the whole concept of the transience of life:

*Yavatpavano/nivasati/dehe*

*Tavatprcchati/kusalam/gehe*

*Gatavati/vayau/dehapaye*

*Bharya/bibhyati/tasminkaye* (6)

'People at your home will show concern for your welfare so long as there is breath in your body. Once the life-breath departs, even your wife will be scared of that body!' Whether it is a husband, wife, or children, the moment the life force leaves one's body, it is called a corpse; people are afraid of even sitting near it. Imagine that the corpse suddenly opens its eyes and sits up. What will happen? The very same wife, who previously embraced that body and took care of all its needs, would now run away, howling "Ghost!!!" Isn't it?

Attachments and nourishments of the body continue until the breath indwells it. The moment the life-breath leaves for good, it becomes inert and inanimate and loses even its former name. It's just a dead body. And, all dead bodies have a common name: corpse.

One's bondage with the body is quite deep. It is the source of all attachments. As Sadhguru says, your deepest sense of attachment is not to your wife/ husband, children, house, or bank balance, as is commonly believed. It is to your own thoughts and emotions. When the persons or things dear to you go against the way you think and feel, what will you be rejecting - the dear ones and things or your thoughts and emotions? You will hold on to your thoughts and emotions, and drop all of the persons or things that go against them. That's the kind of attachment people have with their thoughts and feelings.

Supriya: "How can this problem get addressed?"

Anandavardhan: "Unless experientially it is clear within you that "this body is not me", there's no way you can become unattached from the body. Pan to a story that underscores this point:

## *Indra turns a pig*

Once, Indra, the king of gods, reached Earth looking for some new pastime. He chose the form of a pig to revel in pleasure.

Suhra: "Why a pig, of all living beings?"

Trainer: "Because in terms of physical pleasure, the form of a pig is generally considered the best. Assuming the form of a boar, Indra identified a beautiful sow and took it as his partner. They produced dozens of piglets out of that relationship. Over time, Indra, in his new form got very deeply involved and attached to the sow and the piglets.

The gods waited patiently in heaven, thinking that it was just another short pleasure trip for Indra, as was his wont. But when he didn't return for a long time, they descended over the earth in search of their ruler. They were flabbergasted seeing all the pig business their king got mired in. Devas tried to reason with Indra to give up the life of swine and go with them back to his heavenly abode. But he was so deeply involved and entangled with his pig family that he just grunted and left.

The gods then decided to kill one of the piglets with the hope that the shock of the tragedy would make Indra realize his folly and also his true nature. However, that was not to be. They killed one after all the piglets, only to find that the loss of each piglet made the mourning sire get more and more attached to the rest, and also the dam. Together, the pig pair continued to produce more offspring.

Distressed, the gods then killed the sow herself, which they surmised would end Indra's new *avatar* and the swine-production business.

The death of his partner threw the boar into deep sorrow. His friends and relatives suggested he go for another partner, and the boar did accordingly. The procreation process continued unabated.

The gods were now totally at a loss as to what to do to get back Indra. Fortunately for them, at that time, Narada, the wise sage, who was roaming on earth, happened to pass by that place and saw the gods in a desperate mood. When he understood their predicament, the sage asked: "Why did you kill the sow and the young ones? His attachment is to his body. Destroy that body!" Enlightened, the gods cut the boar's body into two halves. And lo, Indra emerged from the slain body of the pig, exclaiming: "What the hell am I doing here?!" And he trotted back to heaven.

Anandavardhan reverted to the discussion. "We are what we are thanks to the breath within us. A person who breathes 23080 times a day and lives for about 70 years ceases to be the guy who s/he was the moment the breath leaves his/her body. Everything related to his/her identity, including the personal name, position, and power, qualifications, and all becomes alien to him/her at that moment, and the inert body now shares a common name 'corpse'. This is what happens when *jiva* or the life force – *praan shakti* – departs its temporary dwelling place called *kshetra* (vide Bhagavad Gita) or chariot (vide Kattopanishad). It's like checking out a hotel once your stay time thereat is over.

Over to this beautiful story (courtesy: Gauranga Das)

One night, Swami Akinchan Krishna, traveling through the kingdom of Sushant Singh Dogra in

Jammu went to the palace to meet with the king. But the security guards at the gate denied him entry inside on the plea that the king had instructed them not to allow any holy men inside as he was not interested in seeing any beggars.

The swami, who had heard that the king had become morally wayward and had gone attached to women and wine, understood the situation. He was there out of compassion for the citizens of Jammu and wanted to teach the king the path to responsible conduct and behavior. He smiled and said calmly: "I am not here to beg. I came here to give. As it is late in the day, I was just wondering if I could stay here in this big guest house tonight".

Puzzled at the words of a swami, the guards asked: "Guest house? Which guest house are you talking about?

"This big cottage that you are guarding," replied the swami.

The irritated guards got angry and retorted: "Are you mad, old man? This is not any 'big cottage'; this is the royal palace of King Sushant Singh Dogra".

"Don't be foolish. You are mistaken or are mad. Go and ask your king, who is the manager of this hotel, if I can get a room here for tonight".

One of the guards promptly went inside, contemplating that the king would teach this arrogant guy a lesson, and reported that an old beggar monk was mistaking the royal palace for a hotel and insisted that he should get a room for a day.

The king, learning about the visitor, got angry and said: "Bring that idiot here. I'll fix his vision. Daring to insult the royal legacy of the Dogras?!'

The monk was taken to the king. The king asked him: "My guard is saying that you have insulted our royal prestige. Does this palace look like a boarding house for you?"

"Yes. What else? This is a boarding house only," the monk replied calmly and assertively.

Before the angered king could burst out, the monk asked: "O king, tell me, who stayed here before your majesty occupied this?"

'Pointing to a large portrait behind his throne, the king said proudly: "His Royal Majesty King Prashant Singh Dogra, my respected father".

"And before him?" the monk asked again.

Visibly annoyed, the king responded again: "His Royal Highness King Nishant Singh Dogra, my revered grandfather".

The monk ignored the annoyance of the king and demanded to know again: "And before your great grandfather, who was the occupant of this palatial guest house you call a palace, Your Majesty?"

Pointing to a third vintage portrait of his great-grandfather, the king said: "The glory of the Dogra lions, His Excellency King Dishant Singh Dogra."

Looking straight into the king's eyes, the monk asked: "Well, I don't want to know the names of all your forefathers. Just give me this piece of information. Where did all these Majesties, who were the past occupants of this palace, go?"

Puzzled and confused, the king asked: "What do you mean?" This time, his voice was bereft of pride.

"Dear child," the sage answered serenely: "They have all moved onwards, as you also would, one day. They stayed in this magnificent building for a few years each, enjoyed the hospitality, and fought wars to pay their 'rent' for their bed and breakfast, as you do now. Then, with the announcement of their checkout time, they, your predecessors, all had gone, leaving everything behind".

"We are travelers in this life, and we continue our journey in this world until we work our way back home, back to Godhead. Just think it over: Does not your forefathers' stay in this palace sound like a traveller's stay at any guest house?"

The king, shaken and awakened by the deep import of the sage's words, slipped into a reflective mood. Swami continued after a few minutes:

"Son, we are all travelers. We stay within the guest house of our bodies for some time, bearing a name someone gave us, and enjoying the facilities like eating, drinking, and merry-making. We pay our 'rent' by working, feeding, and servicing. Our stay in this body's guest house is limited by time; we have to vacate the house when the sun sets on us.

In other words, when a man exhales and cannot inhale again, he is checking out from the body that was till then his guest house in this world. Later, when he is reborn, he is checked into a new body that will be his new guest house for a predetermined period of occupancy. This is the drama called Life, where we're all actors.

In Bhagavad Gita, Lord Krishna says:

"*vasaamsi/jeernani/yatavihaaya,*
*navaani/grihnaati/naro'paraani,*
*tatha/sareerani/vihaaya/jeernaani,*
*anyani/samyati/navaani/dehee*" (2.22).

The verse means: This body is only like a dress that the *jiva* indwelling you wear. When the dress called the body is old and worn out according to the life force (it may appear to be intact and wearable for the mortal eyes of others, but its quality and usefulness get determined by the *dehee* –the embodied *jiva),* it drops the old dress and takes up a new one.

Like what Swami Akichan Krishna did to the king at the royal palace, Sankaracharya is shaking us vigorously through the verse we studied so that we come out of the mistaken notion that the body is the Self – the *pranashakti.*

And, so the Acharya suggests:
"*Bhaja Govindam.......muda mate....*"

## MAJOR LEARNING POINTS

- ***Indian spirituality was evolved from first-hand experience of rishis of yore, who deduced the truth of Existence through repeated spiritual visions called 'darshan'.***

- **Your deepest sense of attachment is to your own thoughts and emotions.**

- **Human body is the cloth worn by the indwelling jiva. It is compared to a guest house, wherein the soul stays for a pre-determined period.**

# 8

# BEWARE: THIS TOO SHALL PASS

Malathi: “Sir, I have heard that ‘*Bhaja Govindam*’ was earlier known by some other name. What is it?”

Anandavardhan: “The poem was known as *Moha Mudgara*. It literally means: the hammer that destroys ‘moha’ or delusion. All the misery and suffering in the world can be traced to delusion or illusion that arises from wrong perception. When perception goes wrong, we mistake untruth for the truth and unreal for the real.

Sankara tells about the fallacy, folly, and futility of pursuing material pleasures and possessions, which are distractions from the real purpose of life. He removes the veil of illusions and delusions verse by verse and hence the name *Moha Mudgara*.

In the 7th stanza, the Acharya speaks about a universal human nature as people pass through different stages of life.

*"Balastavat/kreedasaktah,*

*Tarunastavat/taruneesaktah;*

*Vriddhastavat/chintasaktah,*

*Parame/brahmani/ko'pina/saktah"*

During childhood, one is attached to play; during the youth, the attachment is to the opposite sex; in the old age, one is immersed in anxieties and worries....... No one gets attached (at any time) to Supreme Brahman!

Life is short. ***The real purpose of human life is realization of the Self, through which only one can attain lasting peace and happiness***. Unfortunately, the veil of 'Maya' is so strong that the deluded humans get engrossed in play during childhood, infatuation as youth, and despondency during the old age. Therefore, the Acharya is saying: "Bhaja Govindam......muda mate" Turn to and seek Govinda.

A fisherman, as usual, went to the river for fishing in the early morning. The sun has not yet risen. As he was leisurely strolling on the river bank, he stumbled upon something heavy. He could understand that it was a bag filled with stones.

Keeping his nest aside, the man squatted on the sand by the side of the bag of stones.

As he was awaiting the day break to start his fishing operation, he casually put his hand inside the nearby bag and took one stone from it. Throwing it to the river he thought: "Here you go, to where you belong" and enjoyed the sound it produced in the still water. He then picked another stone, which also flew to the water. One after the other, the fisherman cast the stones in the bag to the river, alternatively with both the hands, and found it a good exercise for his hands.

By the time the sunlight slowly started to emerge in the east horizon, removing the blanket of darkness that draped the river bank, the fisherman had cast most of the stones into the river. Before throwing away the last piece on hand, he just glanced, for the first time, at the thing he held in his palm, and was shell-shocked. Sparkling in the dim morning light was a precious gem!

Time is like the precious gems in the hands of the fisherman on the river bank. We just waste it thoughtlessly because we are in the dark. Childhood shall give way to adolescence and youth, which also would transit to old age (as Plato cautioned more than 2000 years ago, "fear old age, for it does not come alone"). In life, nothing is permanent. Everything shall pass for something else.

### *'This too shall pass'*

Krishnacharan was a successful and reputed businessman. His only son Mrityunjaya was a talented and resourceful youngster. The father, on reaching above 60, wanted to hand over the business empire to the son and take rest. But the boy expressed his desire to do higher studies abroad. Krishnacharan conceded to the request of Mrityunjaya, who accordingly went to the U.S.A. for his doctoral study.

Before flying abroad, Krishnacharan presented a diamond ring to the son and said: "Look Mrityunjaya. Take this gift, specially made for you. May this ring give you strength of limb and power of mind to weather the storms of life. That's my prayer for you today. I know you don't like to wear a ring. Yet, out of love for me, do wear this. Should you, at any time in the future, feel disheartened and disappointed, go to a quiet corner, sit comfortably, remove the ring from your finger and play with it, tossing it in the air and catching it for a while. This is my parting advice for you. May the household gods, I worship day in and day out, protect you; Godspeed to you".

Mrityunjaya, hardworking and highly intelligent as he was, got the doctorate degree in two years from

America. His circle of friendship and connections had grown by then, and following the suggestions of some well-wishers, he started an industry there itself, with the approval and blessings of his father in India.

Soon he made giant strides in his field and the instruments he manufactured captured the markets in a sweep. His assets grew, as also his brand image. In the fourth year of his operation, however, there was a trade depression which caused a sudden fall in the market value of the goods he had stocked. Soon, there was an unprecedented heavy loss in his business. Mrityunjaya was shocked. Many wealthy partners, who faced their own share of problems, pressed him to return their capital.

He was desperate, disappointed, and dumbfounded. He wondered what his loving father, who had never tasted failure, think of his son if he came to know about his present situation! The conflict within him was so great that in a desperate moment, he thought of ending his life. Late in that night, he drove towards a bridge spanning a mighty river.

The road was deserted. Mrityunjaya got down from the car midway through the bridge, walked towards the railings, stood on top of the railings, ready to plunge headlong into the river. For a while, he began to reminisce. A train of thoughts passed through his mind. He thought of his father and his parting advice. He then looked at his ring the father gifted him on the day of their parting. He had a sudden impulse to satisfy the queer wish of his father before ending his life.

Turning around, he quickly jumped on to the pavement. Finding nobody around, Mrityunjaya spread his kerchief on the pavement under a street lamp. He sat there, removed the ring from his finger and tossed it in the air. As he was repeating the act, suddenly his eye caught sight of an inscription engraved on the inner side of the ring. His heart missed a beat! He had hitherto never bothered to look into the inner side of the ring. Now, his eyes were stuck at the words he read. It said: "EVEN THIS WILL PASS AWAY".

Mrityunjaya pondered for a while. Was this not a message from his father sitting miles and miles away, to take a cue from? Will even this trade depression pass away? Is it just a passing phase only? He had a gut feeling that his father was near him in flesh and blood, asking him not to commit the rash act. He felt the resolve with which he drove to the bridge losing its hold on him.

He got up, jumped into the car, went back to the house, and thought deeply for some time. He had established a name as an honest businessman. The financial institutions in and around the city knew well of his honesty, integrity, and capability. He remembered that many a time they had offered to finance his endeavors. Why not make use of their offers now, he wondered.

He immediately rang up a corporation that he knew worked round the clock and asked if their earlier offer to him still stood. He was delighted to hear that they considered it their privilege to finance him. The next morning, after arranging the funds he immediately required from the corporation he spoke to, he called his partners and said that they could collect their share capital if they wanted. The wonderstruck partners deliberated among themselves and decided to continue the partnership with the indefatigable Mrityunjaya.

With redoubled energy and optimism, he again plunged into the business venture. At the end of the year, he again found himself in clover. His business prospered. Mrityunjaya constantly reminded himself of the message in his ring, "Even this shall pass away". From that deterministic life experience, he learned a valuable lesson and felt a spirit of equanimity deliberating all his actions. ***He understood that he should neither be elated by success nor depressed by failure*** (courtesy: Swami Chinmayananda).

*'This too shall pass' is a great life mantra, an equalizer in life that should be remembered by all, at*

*all times, to have a balanced life. When you are on cloud nine, think that 'this too shall pass'; it would temper your exultation. When you're despondent, this mantra would lift your spirit up and instill hope and optimism within you.*

Now, look at this aphorism 'this too shall pass' from a different perspective. It is generally considered that childhood is for play. Playing the children should, as it is absolutely necessary for their overall development in early years of life. But listen to this: "Science shows that life is a story for which the beginning sets the tone. That makes the formative years of childhood a time of great opportunity and of great risk. Children's brains are built, moment by moment, as they interact with their environments. ***In the first few years of life, more than one million neural connections are formed in their brains each second – a pace never repeated again.*** The quality of a child's early experiences makes a critical difference as their brains develop, providing either strong or weak foundations for learning, health, and behavior throughout life" (unicef.org).

The axiom that 'this too shall pass' should serve as a reminder to discerning parents that **early years of their children's life offer a never-to-be-repeated great opportunity to inculcate in**

**them basics of values, ethics, etc.** A young plant, as Sri Satyasai Baba said, can be bend at your will, but not after its growing to a tree. Swami Vivekananda observed that from childhood onwards, parents teach their children to learn by looking outside, as all our sense organs are created in such a way that they collect signals from outside only. With the result, we never look inside us, which is the repository of the knowledge about the Self and the Almighty.

Similarly, the youth should remember that their (carefree) life with little discipline and responsibility will also come to a pass, and by the time they become aware of it, it would be too late, as old age would set in.

The verse under discussion is a stern reminder to humanity that our time on earth is short, and early in life one should turn towards God. This will be possible by cultivating a discerning and discriminating mind – *viveka* –to distinguish the permanent from the transitory, the real from the unreal so that we can practice dispassion (*vairagya)* from worldly attractions and distractions. By that way only one can we cultivate devotion and realize Govinda, the Absolute Truth, and get released from the misery and bondage of this phenomenal world.

## ***MAJOR LEARNING POINTS***

- ***Lasting peace and happiness can be achieved only through realizing the Self.***

- ***In life, nothing is permanent. Everything shall pass for something else.***

- ***Never get elated by your success or depressed by your failure.***

- ***Science tells that life is a story for which the beginning sets the tone. Early years of children's life provide an excellent, never-to-get-repeated opportunity for sowing in them the seeds of values, ethics, spirituality, etc.***

9

# THE VORTEX OF MAYA

*"Ka/te/kanta/kaste/putrah*

*Samsaro'yamateeva/vichitrah*

*Kasya/tvam/kah/kuta/ayatatah*

*Tattvam/cintaya/tadiha/bhratah*(8)

Who is your wife? Who is your son? Very strange indeed is this 'samsara' (family bond). Whom you belong to? Who are you? From where have you come? Oh, brother! Reflect on the truth of it all.

Sandeep: "Sir, is the Acharya talking here about Maya?"

Anandavardhan: "Yes. A legend is there in which sage Narada once approached Krishna and said: "Lord, show me Maya." After a few days, Krishna asked Narada to join him on a trip to a desert. They started, and after walking for several miles, Krishna said: "Narada, I feel very thirsty. Can you fetch me some water?"

"Sure, master. I will go and get water for you."

Narada went in search of water. After covering some distance, he found a village. He went there and reached a house. He knocked at the door. After a few minutes, the door opened, and he found a beautiful girl standing in front. When he looked at her, Narada forgot everything else, including his purpose of reaching there.

He started to talk with her. Hours passed like that, and Narada failed to return to his master, who was waiting for drinking water.

The following day, he again went to the lass and spent time with her. Their talk ripened into love; Narada asked the girl's father for her hand. He agreed, and they were married. Narada started living there itself. Over time, three children were born to them.

Twelve years went by. His father-in-law died, and Narada inherited his property. He lived a happy and contented life with his wife and the children, looking after their fields, herd of cattle, and so forth. Then one day, there came a flood. The nearby river rose until it overflowed its banks and inundated the entire village. Houses got immersed in incessant flood water. Men and animals were swept away and drowned.

Narada wanted to escape with his dear ones. Getting hold of his wife with one hand, two children with the other, and perching the youngest on his shoulder, he tried to move forward, wading through the rising flood water. After a few steps, he found the current was too strong to withstand. The child on his shoulder fell into the water and got instantly swept away.

A cry of despair arose from Narada. He found that he also was losing his balance, and in the attempt to save the other kids, they slipped from his grasp and flew away. At last, his beloved wife, whom he clasped with all his might, was also mercilessly torn away by the current, and he got thrown on the bank. He wept and wailed in bitter lamentation and utter helplessness.

Behind him, now there came a gentle voice: "My child, where is the water? You went to fetch me a pitcher of water, and I have been waiting for you for the past half an hour".

Narada, who came to his senses, exclaimed: "Half an hour!?" Twelve long years have passed through his mind, and all these scenes had happened in half an hour!!

Krishna smiled and asked: "Where is your wife? Where are your children? What happened to them, Narada? What happened to the property and the cattle you inherited, my boy?"

Krishna continued: "A few days ago, you wanted me to show Maya; and you had a taste of it."

The world we live in is Maya. As observed by Swami Vivekananda, who narrated the above story (CW 2: 120-121), we are all slaves of Maya, born in Maya, and live in Maya. It is against this backdrop, Adi Sankara's words and questions become relevant.

Who is your beloved? Who is your son? Very strange and enigmatic is the world and the bond of relationships we cherish. After all, whom do you belong to and who you are? Wherefrom did you appear in this world? Sankara, addresses the listener as a brother, and suggests him to reflect on these things. The wife and children – none of them was born with you, and none of them would die with you. Nobody accompanies you in birth or death.

You had perhaps never met your wife before marrying her. On a fine day, a lady from somewhere became your better half, your life partner. Who will die first, and then what happens? Who can predict life? As passengers traveling together in a train compartment meeting for the first time, sharing and caring for one another for some time, when your station to disembark arrives, you leave them all. Is not marital and other relationships also like that? Just reflect on it, my brother; think over the truth of this transitory life journey.

And think of your son. Just consider your relationship with him. You became a father after his birth. Before his birth, where was he? In his mother's womb, as an embryo. Before that? There was this sperm within you and the ovum within your wife. Wherefrom did these two come? From the food, both of you ate. And the source of that food? The earth. That means a lump of earth was transformed and evolved through different stages to become the food, the sperm, the ovum, the embryo, the fetus, and the child you call your son. The same is the transitional story behind your birth as well. In other words, we all came from Earth and will return to Earth.

Sankara is saying: One lump of transformed earth is calling another lump of earth its own, and they love and care for each other as if they came together and would go back together. Can anything be stranger than this? A bizarre play of Maya indeed!

## *Who am I?*

Ramana Maharshi clarified and answered the question: "Who am I?" The purpose of asking this question is to withdraw the mind from wandering in the outer world and to make it dive deep into one's Self. The monkey mind, nothing but a bundle of thoughts, will eventually vanish through constant meditation on the question: Who am I?

Why we are unhappy in life? Sri Ramana maintains that this is because we fail to appreciate our true nature, which is happiness and is inborn in the True Self. The reality is that ***the constant urge of all of us to secure happiness in life is an unconscious search for our True Self.***

We are our minds, and the mind consists of thoughts. 'I' thought is the first thought produced by the mind. When the 'I' thought is earnestly pursued by the inquiry 'Who am I?' and followed up, all the other thoughts will get destroyed. Finally, the 'I' thought also will disappear, leaving the supreme non-dual 'Self' alone. The false identification of the Self with the phenomenon of non-self, viz., the body and the mind, thus ends, and there is illumination (*sakshatkara).*

For the mind that has acquired the skill to concentrate, self-inquiry is relatively easy. The thoughts are destroyed by ceaseless inquiry, and the

Self stands realized. All living beings long to be happy at all times, without any misery. There is observed supreme love for oneself within everyone. And happiness alone is the cause of love. Therefore, to gain that happiness, which is one's nature and which we all experience in the state of deep sleep where there's no mind, one should seek to know oneself. To achieve this, the Path of Knowledge, the inquiry in the form of 'who am I', is the principal means.

Through the verse, Sri Sankara is suggesting not to confuse the body, which is perishable, with the soul, which is imperishable, and not to be a victim of attachments. Kattopanishad says:

"*Paraanchi/khani/vyatrinat/swayambhuhu,*
*tasmat/paraan/pashyati/naantaratman.......*

(2.4.1).

It means, God has created the sense organs as outward-bound and therefore the human mind can engage itself in the objects of the outer world only. Therefore, if you want to know who you are, redirect your attention and concentrate on the inner Self. When that is actualized, all the delusions and illusions will vanish forever.

## MAJOR LEARNING POINTS

- *We are all slaves of Maya. Our origin can be traced to the five Elements, starting with Earth. We come from Earth and return to Earth. All our sense of possessiveness in life stems from the play of Maya.*

- *The constant urge of all of us to secure happiness in life is an unconscious search for our True Self.*

- *We are our thoughts, and our thoughts begin with the 'I' thought. When the 'I' thought is persistently pursued, all other thoughts will disappear, and finally, the 'I' thought too will vanish.At that moment, the non-dual Self will shine forth, answering the question: "Who am I?" And, that is 'sakshatkara'.*

- *Who you are can be found out by redirecting your attention to the inner Self, and concentrating on it until it is realized.*

# 10

# LADDER OF DELIVERANCE

Malathi: "Sir, if most of the people are hankering for worldly pleasures, despite knowing that such things are incapable of offering eternal peace and happiness, is it not because of their inherent *vasanas*, which, as I understand it, is born out of past karmas?"

Trainer: "You have a valid point there, Malathi. Let's understand *vasana* first. It is a technical term in Indian philosophy, and the word means 'to remain', 'to dwell', 'to persist' (in memory), etc. Most often, vasana is associated with the notion of desires. ***Vasanas are our inherent latencies and tendencies resulting from our previous actions.*** They govern the psyche and assume the form of predispositions, tendencies, or propensities of the mind in the present life, which have their genesis in the experiences of the past lives".

Sandeep: "What is the difference between vasana and habit?"

Trainer: "What we do with our body, mind, and energy will leave a certain imprint that becomes our tendencies and habits. This is what we generally call vasana."

Lal: "We also call smell a vasana. Is it the same vasana you talked about?

Anandavardhan: "Yes. Each of us has a unique smell that we send out. Sadhguru terms it the 'smell of bondage' because depending on the nature of smell we emanate, we attract certain kinds of life situations to ourselves. The smell you emit is produced by a vast accumulation of impressions caused by your physical, mental, emotional, and energy actions.

Says Sadhguru: "If you exude a particular kind of vasana, Existence will ensure you land up in certain places at certain times. If the smell exuded is different, the universe will make sure that you land up in certain other places. So, ***what moves towards you and what moves away from you is determined by the smell or vasana you send out***.

In other words, vasana is born out of past karma. All the impressions of past lives accumulated in the human mind will transform into a tendency. It is an inclination or disposition to move in a particular direction or act in a certain way. A large number of these impressions on the mind will crystalize and become a habit, which is the outward manifestation of your 'samskara'."

Supriya: "So far, through the discussion on the Bhaja Govindam verses, I was wondering why people madly go after worldly parameters and end up in suffering and misery, notwithstanding the cautions and indoctrinations contained in the texts like the Gita, Bhaja Govindam, and others. Now, things are getting clearer to me. It is the karmic imprint or inherent vasanas which influence and direct a person's behavior."

Anandavardhan: "Good observation, Supriya. Sankara shows the way to get out of this conundrum in the next verse, which is:

*"Satsangatve/nissangatvam,*
*nissangatve/nirmohatvam*

*Nirmohatve/nischalatattvam,*
*nischalatattve/jivanmukti"*

*(9)*

Through the company of the wise, (there arises) non-attachment. Through non-attachment, (there arises) freedom from delusion. When there is freedom from delusion, there is unchangeable reality. On experiencing unchangeable reality, there comes liberation or freedom

## LADDER OF DELIVERANCE

All good and bad actions of the past, which have left their karmic imprints and become our tendencies and habits, come to fruition at the right time and in the right environment. The root cause of your suffering is the seed tendencies within you that have come from your past life-behavior. These seeds sprout under the right conditions and environment.

That explains why it is always important to mix with good company. Unfortunately, people accord scant importance to selecting their friends. They may be principled and may also be conscious of values. But the inherent vasanas compel them to seek fulfillment of desires for which they often choose a bad company. We don't know what kinds of seeds, whether of diseases or other negative happenings, lie dormant within us. So it is very unwise to mix with bad people, for the latent seeds of wrong actions and behavior, carried within our consciousness, are waiting for the right environment to germinate and come up.

**This path of overcoming fate or karma is the most promising philosophy as it proves that the locus of control of your life is well within you; you are the architect of your life.**

Thomas: "But how to overcome bad tendencies and vasanas?"

Trainer: "Let me explain. Each of your habits creates a specific groove or pathway in your brain. These patterns cause you to behave in a certain way, often against your wish (that's why you choose to mix with people of low morals). Your life follows these grooves that you have created in the brain.

But the flip side is that you can neutralize the dictates of these bad habits. For the purpose, you have to create brain patterns of opposite (good) habits. It is within your power to completely erase the grooves of bad habits by meditation. However, you cannot cultivate good habits without *satsanga* and a good environment conducive to meditation.

The verse says: Company of the good roots out all attachments. When there is no attachment, there is no delusion/desire. No delusion means the mind is steady. A steady mind makes for *jivanmukti*. To rephrase it, association with good and pious people helps to reduce and eliminate infatuation. In the absence of infatuation, the person attains equanimity and divine peace. These come one after the other, like leaves, flowers, and fruit in a tree. Or, these are the ascending steps of a ladder – the ladder of deliverance.

As desires and attachments become less and less, thanks to *satsanga,* the delusion that destroys the power of discrimination between the good and the bad, between the lofty and the low, disappears. When that happens, the mind ceases to be agitated (with desires and attachments) and becomes steady. When the mind becomes steady, it leads to internal purity, the characteristics of *Sivam,* the Divinity. Reaching that state is *jivanmukti* –Self-realization.

Sandeep: "But, is not jivanmukti a state to aspire for attainment after one's physical death?"

Trainer: "No. It's a wrong notion entertained by many people. ***He who has the direct experience of the Self is known as liberated even while he is still alive. Such a person is known as jivanmukta.*** It is not a state to be aspired and attained after death. *Jivanmuktas* are the 'living incarnations of the Truth and their very existence renders the Truth demonstrable' In *Vivekachdamani* (verse 429) AdiSankara says: "***He who has steady wisdom, who experiences endless Bliss, who has forgotten the phenomenal world, he is considered a jeevan-mukta.***" 'We are all living in the realm of PFT (Perceiver- Feeler- Thinker), the *jiva* identified with the BMI (Body-Mind -Intellect), and the OET (Objects –Emotions –Thoughts). ***Jeevan-mukti* is liberation from the concept of jeeva-**

***hood***. He who has transcended the concept of the PFT, who has no identification with his BMI, is called the liberated one. L**iberated he is, from the lower because of his awakening to the Higher**. When one has transcended all the instruments and their objects, pure Knowledge is sinks in. According to the Rishis, this is *Kaivalya'*.

***Satsanga – nissanga –nirmoha -nischalatatva– jeevanmukti****:* This is how the ladder of deliverance operates. In contra, Bhagavad Gita talks about another ladder –the ladder of destruction. It will be instructive to juxtapose both the ladders. Over to the Gita slokas:

*Dhyayato/vishayan/pumsah*

Sangasteshupajayate

*Samgat/samjayate/kamah*

*Kamat/krodho'bhijayate*

*(2.62)*

When we think about a sense object continuously, the consistency of that thought creates within us an attachment towards that object. As more and more thoughts start flowing towards the object of attachment, they crystalize to form a burning desire for its possession and enjoyment. If any obstacle stands in the way of the realization/attainment of the desired object, the motion directed at the (desired) object gets re-directed, with the same intensity, to such obstacles in the form of anger.

And then what happens?

*Krodhat/bhavati/sammohah*

*Sammohat/smritivibhramah*

*Smritibhramsat/buddhinaso*

*Buddhinasat/pranasyati*

*(2.63)*

When anger builds up, the intellect starts to fall into delusion. Delusion causes the loss of power of discrimination. When the power of discrimination is lost, a person forgets the self, his relationship with the others, and he ventures into indulging in actions that he won't dare do in a steady mental state. This happens because his sense of proportion is lost, his dignity of culture forgotten, and his conscience (*Buddhi*) also is alienated. Once the conscience is dulled, his final fall –destruction – ensues. Here, the play of PFT and OET causes the progressive ruin of BMI and attracts the worst consequences.

In short, ***the steps in the ladder of destruction are object –attachment – desire – anger – delusion - loss of discriminative power and memory - loss of conscience - the***

***ultimate fall***. We can see that compared to the ascending ladder of deliverance, there are more steps on the descending ladder of destruction, and the person stoops to a stupefying low.

So, what to do? *Bhaja Govindam……muda mate*. All that we hold dear in life, the material possessions and acquisitions for which we waste our short and precious lifetime, will either be lost or have to be renounced at some time or other. The Acharya says that it is only through Brahma vidya one can escape the clutches of Maya. The first step to ascending that ladder of deliverance is *satsanga*.

## MAJOR LEARNING POINTS

- ***Vasana is born out of one's past karmas. It is an inclination to move in a particular direction or act in a certain way.***

- **The locus of control of your life is within you; you're the architect of your life.**

- **Satsanga – association with the good and pious people – is the first step in the ladder of deliverance.**

- **He who has the direct experience of the Self is called the liberated, even when he is alive. He is the jivan-mukta.**

- **Only through Brahma Vidya, one can escape the clutches of Maya.**

# 11

# BE A LION, NOT A DOG'

A son was born to a rich merchant in a south Indian village after waiting for long. He grew as a much-pampered boy, and led a carefree life of indulgence. As he grew up, he had a lot of friends who filled his life with merry-making parties and extravagance. On attaining marriageable age, he received proposals from parents of beautiful and rich girls.

He got married, and everything went great for quite some time. He spent his father's fortune carelessly and endlessly, and his swelling friends were having a heyday with him. As it is said, everything has an exit-time, and this man became bankrupt on a fateful day. He turned to his friends for support and assistance, but they all avoided him mercilessly. When money left him, not only his friends, but his dear wife and children also deserted him. They didn't want to stay with an insolvent and ruined man.

The man, who till then was always surrounded by friends and relatives, suddenly found himself lonely and disheartened. His health deteriorated, and he resorted to all bad habits and vices. As a result, before long, he became bedridden. During this time, the man started reflecting on his past and how he spent his youthfulness and resources. He understood that his attachments to material objects, friends and relatives, wife and children, all was a sheer waste and that he was a total failure in life.

He decided to end his life, but fate had other plans for him. One day, a wandering monk visited him. Saints come to one's life by the grace of God. Seeing the pathetic state of the man, the monk took him to his ashram. There, the inmates took care of his needs.

After a few weeks, when his physical and mental conditions improved, the man sought the permission of the monk to stay in the ashram and serve the inmates and the guru. The master smiled and advised him: "My dear, be a Lion, not a dog."

The man didn't understand its meaning. The guru asked: "When you throw a ball in front of a dog, what will the dog do?"

"The dog will run after the ball and fetch it for you," replied the man.

"Okay. When you throw a ball in front of a Lion, what will it do?"

"It will chase you, not the ball," said the man.

"All these years," said the monk, "you behaved like a dog and chased the temporary pleasures the life threw on your path. You didn't try to reflect on real and permanent Truth of life. Now that you have understood your folly in a hard and bitter way, shift your focus and attention to what is real and permanent in life. You'll be much better and happier".

The man felt grateful to the master for opening his eyes. He started living a pious life in the ashram and became happy, healthy, and contented. He soon realized that this world is impermanent; he had to seek something higher and the ultimate. He soon turned into a diligent and devoted disciple.

The master watched his progress and transformation closely. Impressed with his fast evolutionary changes, the monk decided to anoint him as his heir at the ashram. Accordingly, he was initiated into monkhood on an auspicious day, and the man took charge of the ashram and its activities. Over time, he started imparting knowledge of truth and wisdom to all the devotees and disciples. (Courtesy: saibalasankaar. wordpress.com)

Trainer: "Let's now listen to what Sri Sankara has to say about this phenomenon of human life:

*"Vayasi/gate /kah/kamavikarah*

*Suske/neere/kah/kasaarh*

*Ksheene/vitte/kah/parivaro*

*Jnate/tatve/kah/samsarah"*

(10)

When youth is gone, of what use is lust? Where is the lake, when the water has dried up? Where is one's retinue when the wealth is gone? When the Truth is realized, where is *samsara* (the worldly bond)?

How can there be a display of lust, if the youthfulness is no more? ***There cannot be an effect without an underlying cause***. Youthfulness is a cause, and an expression of lust is the effect the cause produces. The idea is that when the cause is not there, the effect will automatically disappear.

A body of water is known as a lake, a pond, or a river till such time it is filled with water. Once the water gets dried up, as it happens in the summer season in many parts of the country, where is the lake, pond, or river? Similarly, if you lose your wealth, where is your family or retinue? People are around you only when they find that you can offer them something or they want to gain something from their association with you.

Don't be fooled. Identify the real cause for any effect to accrue, and don't be carried away simply by the effect. ***Sorrow and suffering haunt you only so long as the mind is deluded.*** When delusion vanishes, the sorrow and suffering wane like mist before the sun. How can the delusion get removed? -only through wisdom.

We seem to be swept away by the flow of life and the direction of its current, and in the process, lose sight of our focus on the true goal, which is to acquire knowledge about the Self. Even the most persistent sorrows and cares will vanish with the dawn of true knowledge of Self. What we experience in daily life is the relative truth, which is the cause of our ups and downs, joys and sorrows. To realize the ultimate and permanent truth, the only way before us is to contemplate and look within ourselves till we become Self-realized.

Supriya: "Sir, what's the meaning of the last line of the verse: "*Jnate/tatve/kah/samsarah?*"

Trainer: "That is the most noteworthy part of this verse. We are all interested in acquiring freedom from the samsara. What is samsara? '*Samyak/sarati/ asmin/iti/samsarah*'. The word samsara can be understood by splitting it into two – *sam* and *sara*. *Sara* is derived from *sr* –to move. Sarati is the one who moves. *Sam* comes from *samyak,* meaning constant. *Samsara* – *samyak/sara*- means that in which there is incessant movement.

Sandeep: "What kind of movement does it signify?"

Anandavardhan: "It is the movement from one birth to another, from one stage or situation to another, from one accomplishment to some other, and the like. Man, by nature, always strives to become something. This life of becoming is called samsara."

Lal: "If one strives for accomplishment of something or to become somebody, is it not a virtue? Why should we seek freedom from such movement, which perhaps is a positive attribute of human nature?"

Trainer: "Please understand that no material accomplishment or achievement will be long-lasting or help realize the ultimate goal of life. Going after material pursuits is a shift in focus from the eternal to the transient, which acts as an obstacle to self-realization. Therefore, we have to seek freedom from samsara. In reality, the only freedom that we have to acquire is inner freedom."

That's why Sri Sankara asks: *Jnate/tatve/kah/ samsara?* When the *tatva* or truth is known, where is samsara, your worldly bond? Here, truth means the truth of Self, the ignorance of which is the cause of samsara. When can the truth be known? As stated in the previous sloka, *nirmohatve/nischala/tatva*. The truth can be perceived only when the mind is free from *raga-dweshas*-likes and dislikes- so that the mind is enabled to see it.

This clarity is gained only upon surrender to the Almighty God. Therefore, the Acharya asserts: "*Bhaja Govindam, bhaja Govindam......muda mate.*"

(Courtesy: Swami ViditatmanandaJi)

The essence of the verse is that the sorrows of life will cease to exist upon the realization of knowledge of the Self. The cause of all our sorrows is ignorance of the true self. If we can remove the cause, the effect will be gone, and we will no longer be victims of samsara. What we are doing today in daily life is fighting the effect without removing the cause. By doing so, we may change something for a while, but it will recur for sure.

## MAJOR LEARNING POINTS

- ***Nothing happens in the world without a cause. When the cause disappears, the effect also vanishes.***

- ***Wisdom is in identifying the real cause of any effect that accrues, and dealing with it, applying diligence and judiciousness.***
- ***Delusion of the mind is the cause of all the sorrows and sufferings.***

- ***'Samsara' signifies incessant movement – from birth to birth, from state to state, etc.***

- ***Ignorance of Self is the cause of samsara.***

## ACKNOWLEDGMENTS

As Kabir Das, a 15th-century Indian mystic poet and saint, famously said, the Guru first. The spiritual enlightenment, in the most limited and loose sense of the word, I could gain through the long and close association with my Guru, Navajyothisree Karunakaraguru, a Master non-pareil, has facilitated my author-journey through my books immensely. The nuggets of wisdom that knocked at the door of my imagination as I wrote the pages of my books were amazing, as these never occurred to me till the moments of truth arrived! That's the power of Guru. I mentally prostrate at thy feet, Master.

I am beholden to the renowned authors and other scholars whose works came in handy for me to gain insights into the different perspectives of the topic of this book.

My thanks are due to my mentor SomBathla, my colleague Chandralekha (for her support in formatting the book), and N. Sareej, whose creative mind has brought out beautiful and impressive covers for all my books.

Finally, not because you're the last in the queue, but because, as the consumer of the final product, you appear in the picture only after the above-named, I sincerely thank you, the reader of this book, and all the readers and reviewers of my earlier titles. Your encouragements and support have been the fuel in my creative journey. From the bottom of my heart, I thank you for the kind gesture, extended and anticipated (for my future works).

# BIBLIOGRAPHY

Asim Chaudhuri (2011). Vivekananda, A Born Leader. Swami Bodhasarananda Adhyaksha Advaita Ashrama, Mayavati Champawat, Uttarakhand 262524

Chinmayananda, Swami (1981). Talks on Sankara's Vivekachoodamani. Central Chinmaya Mission Trust, Powai-Park-Drive, Mumbai- 400072

Chinmayananda, Swami (1989). Parables. Central Chinmaya Mission Trust Publications, Sandeepany Sadhanalaya, Powai Park Drive, Mumbai-400072

Chinmayananda, Swami (2011). Bhaja Govindam (Malayalam). Chinmaya Publications, CCMT, 'Sreyas', Chinmaya Seva Trust, Ernakulam, Kerala, India-682016

Gauranga Das (2021). The Art of Resilience. Penguin Random House India Pvt. Ltd., 7th Floor, Infinity Tower C, DLF Cyber City, Gurgaon, Haryana-122002

Rajagopalachari C (2017). Bhaja Govindam. Bharatiya Vidhya Bhavan, Kulapati K.M. Munshi Marg, Mumbai-400007

Ranganathananda, Swami (1993). 'Social Responsibilities of Public Administrators'; in Eternal Values for a

Changing Society Vol.IV; Democracy for Total Human Fulfilment. Bharatiya Vidhya Bhavan, Mumbai.

Sadhguru (2021).Karma: A Yogi's Guide to Crafting Your Destiny. Harmony Books, Random House, Penguin Random House LLC, New York.

Sukhabodhananda, Swami (2012). Bhaja Govindam: Seeking and Finding Answers Within. Jaico Publishing House, A-2, Jash Chambers,7-A Sir Phirozshah Mehta Road, Fort, Mumbai- 400001

Sri M (2010). Apprenticed to a Himalayan Master A Yogi's Autobiography. Magenta Press and Publication Pvt. Ltd., Cauvery Towers, Kodagu, Karnataka 571201

## A REQUEST TO THE READER

May I entreat you, my esteemed reader, for a small favor?

First, kindly accept my deep sense of gratitude to you for having bought and read this book. This is the first of the three volumes in a new series proposed to be produced on a Classic by Sri Sankara, wherein he has encapsulated the substance of all his *Vedaantic* works. I shall be obliged if you could provide me with your valuable rating and a review of the book on the Amazon site. Such a small gesture from your side would be a great support, inspiration, and encouragement for me in my author journey, where I find my passion and mission.

I shall be deeply obliged if you would also get, read, and review my highly rated and much acclaimed other titles, including a 5-book-series named 'Gems of Mahabharata' anda 3-Volume series on ‘The Art of Man-Making’, many of which have been multiple times international # 1 bestsellers in the U.S.A., the U.K., Australia, and India (a mention of my 12 books is there at the outset of this book).

Thanks, once again.

www.ingramcontent.com/pod-product-compliance
Lightning Source LLC
LaVergne TN
LVHW091106150826
845673LV00002B/736

* 9 7 9 8 8 9 2 7 7 4 6 8 0 *